GREAT EXPLORATIONS

LEWIS AND CLARK

from Ocean to Ocean

HAROLD FABER

BENCHMARK BOOKS

MARSHALL CAVENDISH
NEW YORK

With Special thanks to Stephen Pitti, Yale University,
for his careful reading of this manuscript.

Benchmark Books
Marshall Cavendish Corporation
99 White Plains Road
Tarrytown, New York 10591-9001

Copyright © 2002 by Harold Faber
Maps by Rodica Prato
All rights reserved.
No part of this book may be reproduced in any form without written permission of the publisher.

Library of Congress Cataloging-in-Publication Data
Harold Faber, date
Lewis and Clark: Ocean to Ocean / by Harold Faber
p. cm. – (Great explorations)
Includes bibliographical references and index.
ISBN 0-7614-1241-7
1. Lewis and Clark Expedition (1804-1806)—Juvenile literature. 2. West (U.S.)—Discovery and exploration—
Juvenile literature. 3. West (U.S.)—Description and travel—Juvenile literature. [1. Lewis and Clark Expedition
(1804-1806) 2. West (U.S.)—Discovery and exploration.] I. Title. II. Series.
F592.7 .F33 2001   917.804'2—dc21   00-051898

Cover photo: Corbis/Bettmann
Photo research by Candlepants Incorporated
The photographs in this book are used by permission and through the courtesy of; *The Denver Public Library,
Western History Division* : title page, 40, 58-59. *Art Resource* : Reunion des Musees Nationaux, 6, 11; Smithsonian
American Art Museum, 12-13, 32; Werner Forman, 57. *Virginia Military Institute Museum* : 14. *Culver Pictures* :
18. *Saint Charles County Historical Society* : 23. *Corbis* : 26; Bettmann, 8, 28; Geoffrey Clements, 66; Macduff
Everton, 70; *The Montana Historical Society* : 36, 51. *Joslyn Art Museum, Omaha, Nebraska* : 42. *Peabody Museum,
Harvard University* : 45. *The Missouri Historical Society* : 47. *The Thomas Gilcrease Institue of American History
and Art, Tulsa, Oklahoma* : 48, 50, 53, 64. National Portrait Gallery/Smithsonian Institution/Art Resource, NY: 16.
Smithsonian American Art Museum, Washington, DC/Art Resource, NY: 31.

Printed in Hong Kong
1 3 5 6 4 2

Contents

Lewis and Clark on the Columbia River, with Toussaint
Charbonneau and Sacagawea, carrying her son.

foreword

In the year 1800, when Thomas Jefferson was elected the third president, the United States was a small country. It stretched from the Atlantic Ocean in the east to the Mississippi River in the west, from the Great Lakes and the St. Lawrence River in the north almost to the Gulf of Mexico in the south.

Three years later that changed. With the Louisiana Purchase in 1803, the United States doubled in size, from 847,335 square miles (1.4 million square kilometers) to 1.7 million square miles (2.7 million square kilometers). The Louisiana Purchase stretched the United States far west, to the border of lands owned by Spain in the southwest and California and to the edge of the disputed Oregon Territory on the Pacific Ocean.

For far-sighted Americans like Jefferson, the vision of the United States growing from sea to sea—from the Atlantic to the Pacific—seemed likely to come to pass.

But what was out there?

Except for the trading villages of St. Louis in the north and New

Flags being changed in New Orleans as the Louisiana Territory
is transferred to the United States in 1803.

Orleans in the south, the new lands of the United States were largely unknown territory. Who lived there? What kinds of animals and plants were there? Could there be a river to provide an easy passage for commercial traffic to the Pacific Ocean and beyond?

To find out, Jefferson planned an exploratory expedition. He called upon his young assistant, Meriwether Lewis, to lead it.

O N E

Meriwether Lewis

Meriwether Lewis got his unusual first name from his mother, who was Lucy Meriwether before her marriage to William Lewis. The marriage united two large landowning families in Albemarle County, not far from Charlottesville, Virginia. Their second child, born on August 18, 1774, was named Meriwether Lewis.

Before he was a year old, his father left to serve in the Continental Army during the Revolutionary War. The boy never got to know his father, who died in 1779 from pneumonia.

He, his older sister, Jane, and younger brother, Reuben, grew up in comfortable circumstances on a large farm. The nearby hills and mountains were full of bears, deer, and wild turkeys. By the time he was eight years old, Meriwether was an experienced hunter.

Meriwether sharpened his hunting skills when his mother and her second husband, Captain John Marks, moved to the Georgia frontier in

Meriwether Lewis on the trail.

1783. As the older son, he was to inherit the large family estate in Virginia, Locust Hill, but he was obviously too young to manage it. So one of his uncles took over while the family lived in Georgia.

Meriwether learned to read and write in Georgia. When he was thirteen, his mother decided that he needed a more formal education—he was, after all, the son of a gentleman and the owner of a large estate. So in 1787 he returned to Virginia.

At that time, there were no public schools in Virginia. Like other sons of well-off families, Meriwether got his education by boarding with teachers, usually ministers. His schooling consisted of Latin, mathematics, natural sciences, and English grammar.

One of his classmates described him:

Always remarkable for perseverance . . . a martial temper; great steadiness of purpose, self possession and undaunted courage. His person was stiff and without grace, bow-legged, awkward, formal, and almost without flexibility. His face was comely, and by many considered handsome.

By the time he was eighteen, his formal education was complete. He returned to Locust Hill, where he was the master of two thousand acres of farmland and twenty-four slaves working the fields. The year was 1792, a time when slavery was an accepted way of life in the South.

Despite his youth, Lewis managed the plantation very well. But the life of a Virginia gentleman did not satisfy him. When President George Washington called state militia to help in putting down the Whiskey Rebellion in Pennsylvania in 1794, Lewis joined up. Even though there was no fighting, Lewis was recognized as a promising soldier. He was quickly promoted to the rank of ensign, then lieutenant, and after a few years to captain.

In his years as a soldier, Lewis traveled extensively. As a paymaster for the army, he went by horseback and by canoe to forts along the

Ohio River, bringing the soldiers their pay. It was an education in wilderness travel that would be extremely helpful in the years ahead.

His life changed dramatically in 1801 when his neighbor in Virginia, Thomas Jefferson, became president of the United States. Jefferson wrote to Lewis that he needed a private secretary,

> *not only to aid in the private concerns of the household, but also to contribute to the mass of information which it is interesting for the administration to acquire. Your knolege of the Western country, of the army and of all its interests & relations has rendered it desirable . . . that you should be engaged in that office.*

Lewis eagerly accepted.

Lewis reported for work in Washington on April 1, 1801. He was twenty-six years old, thrust into the center of the nation's government.

At the President's Mansion (it was not yet called the White House), Lewis lived and worked as a member of Jefferson's family. Not only was he a secretary, he was Jefferson's chief personal aide. He helped with correspondence, arranged dinners for foreign diplomats, and attended conferences with members of Congress and the cabinet.

During two years of close association, Lewis became acquainted with Jefferson's intense interest in the West. At that time, the area beyond the Mississippi River was largely unexplored territory. Four European nations had interests in the region. Great Britain had pushed west toward the Pacific in Canada and down into Oregon. Spain controlled the entire Southwest, as well as the Louisiana territory and the port of New Orleans. France contested the Spanish presence in Louisiana. And Russia had extended her ownership of Alaska south toward the Columbia River.

Jefferson saw that vast area as a potential part of a growing United

In 1801, the presidential residence was called the President's Mansion.
It would not be called the White House for some time.

States. With a vision of America stretching from sea to shining sea, he set out to help the nation expand.

His vague thoughts about gaining a foothold in the West crystallized in 1802 because of a book written by a young Scotsman, Alexander Mackenzie. A fur trader in Canada, Mackenzie in 1793 became the first European to cross the continent north of Mexico and reach the Pacific Ocean. In his book, Mackenzie urged Britain to develop that route as a gateway to the Pacific and trade with Asia.

For Jefferson, this was a warning: if he did not act soon, the entire Northwest might come under British control. He decided that it was time for the United States to establish its claim to the West. To do so, he proposed an expedition to the Pacific Ocean—even though the United States did not yet own any territory west of the Mississippi River.

In his own household was just the man to lead that expedition— Meriwether Lewis.

Jefferson explained why he picked Lewis in a letter to a friend:

Capt. Lewis Is brave, prudent, habituated to the woods, & familiar with Indian matters & character. He is not regularly educated, but he possesses a great mass of accurate observation on all subjects of nature which present themselves here.

Lewis moved quickly in the early part of 1803 to prepare for the expedition.

He went to Philadelphia for short courses in medicine, celestial observation, botany, mapmaking, and fossils. At the army's arsenals in Philadelphia and Harper's Ferry, he obtained rifles, a cannon, and ammunition. For his men, he bought tools, mosquito nets, fishing hooks

and lines, blankets, hooded coats, even 150 pounds (68 kilograms) of a "portable soup," a paste made from boiled beef, eggs, and vegetables. He ordered a riverboat and two canoes to be built in Pittsburgh.

As gifts for the Indians he would meet, he bought twelve dozen pocket mirrors, 4,600 sewing needles, silk ribbons, ivory combs, handkerchiefs, brightly colored cloth, tomahawks, 130 rolls of tobacco, eight brass kettles, scissors, awls for making moccasins, and thirty-three pounds of beads.

Lewis also got his final instructions from Jefferson:

The object of your mission is to explore the Missouri River & such principal stream of it, as, by its course and communications with the waters of the Pacific Ocean, whether the Columbia, Oregon, Colorado or any other river, may offer the most direct and practicable water communication across this Continent for the purposes of commerce.

He emphasized that even though the expedition was an army

Fur traders bargaining with Indians.

Model of the rifle carried by Lewis and Clark and their men.

---

enterprise, it was to be a peaceful one. "In all your intercourse with the natives, treat them in the most friendly and conciliatory manner which their conduct will admit," he said.

Only one thing remained before his departure: recruiting the men to serve under him and an officer to be his assistant. Lewis knew just the man he wanted, Captain William Clark, with whom he had served years before. He wrote to Clark, offering to make him not second in command, but an equal commander with him, adding:

If therefore there is anything under those circumstances, in this enterprise, which would induce you to participate with me in it's fatiegues, it's dangers, and it's honors, believe me, there is no man on earth with whom I should feel equal pleasure in sharing them as with yourself.

T W O

William Clark

William Clark came from a family of warriors. He was only a boy during the Revolutionary War, but his brothers were active in the Continental Army. His oldest brother, Jonathan, was a major in the Virginia militia. Another brother, John, was taken prisoner by the British. His most famous brother, George Rogers Clark, was a general in the Continental Army, serving with distinction on the western frontier.

William was born on August 1, 1770, on a large plantation in Caroline County, Virginia. The ninth child of John and Ann Clark, he grew up in comfortable circumstances on the farm, with many slaves doing the fieldwork. During his childhood, his constant companion was a black slave about his age named York.

Because there were no public schools in rural Virginia, Will had little formal schooling. He never did learn to spell.

After the Revolution, in 1784, the Clark family moved west, to the

William Clark in his later years.

frontier in Kentucky. Will's father built a large house on a farm outside Louisville called Mulberry Hill. Will grew up there, strong and tall, reaching a height of over six feet. Later the Indians would name him Red Head because of his bright red hair.

At the age of sixteen, he accompanied his brother, General Clark, on an expedition against hostile Indians. In the years that followed, he served as a cadet on several other army missions. One of his commanders praised him in a letter to his brother. "He is a youth of solid and promising parts and as brave as Caesar." Will liked army life and served so well that in 1792, he received a commission as a lieutenant.

Three years later Clark was a captain commanding a group of sharpshooters under General Anthony Wayne. For six months, one of his junior officers was Ensign Meriwether Lewis. In that time, the two men got to know and respect each other's character and ability.

Clark, who was four years older than Lewis, got along easily with the soldiers under him. He became adept at living in the wilderness, experienced in handling boats, and an expert mapmaker—all skills that would come in handy later.

In 1796, their paths separated. Lewis remained in the army, but Clark resigned. He made his home in Clarksville, Indiana, a tiny settlement across the Ohio River from Louisville, Kentucky. In 1803, he received the letter from Meriwether Lewis that changed his life. He answered immediately:

> *Dear Lewis,*
> *as my situation in life will admit of my absence the length of time necessary to accomplish such an undertaking, I will cheerfully join you. . . . This is an immense undertaking fraited with numerous difficulties, but My friend I can assure you that no man lives with whom I would prefer to undertake and share the Difficulties of such a trip than yourself.*
>
> *William Clark*

Seaman, Lewis's constant companion.

Thus began one of the most remarkable partnerships in American history.

Lewis came down the Ohio River from Pittsburgh in a newly constructed boat. With him were a river pilot, ten men as possible recruits, and his companion, Seaman, a large black Newfoundland dog.

He met Clark in October 1803 in Clarksville. Their first job was to select the members of their crew. Although it was to be a military expedition, the two officers knew they needed civilian help, as well as soldiers—reliable boatmen, scouts, hunters, and interpreters. Clark had already decided that one of those civilians would be York, his slave.

More than one hundred men had applied to become soldiers in the expedition, but Lewis and Clark chose only nine, based on their hunting ability, physical strength, and character. In a solemn ceremony, they were inducted into the army, and the Corps of Discovery—the unit's official name—came into being.

They left Clarksville on October 26. En route down the Ohio River

A ROLL CALL

Following is a roster of the men who accompanied Lewis and Clark to the Pacific Ocean, as submitted by Lewis to Congress for payment in 1807. Notable by their absence are the names of Sacagawea, the only woman on the expedition, and York, the only black on the expedition, a sign of the prejudices of their time.

Sergeants: John Ordway, Nathaniel Pryor, Patrick Gass, and Charles Floyd (who died en route).

Privates: William Bratton, John Collins, John Colter, Pierre Cruzatte, Joseph Field, Reuben Field, Robert Frazier, Silas Goodrich, George Gibson, Thomas P. Howard, Hugh Hall, Francis Labuiche, Hugh M'Neal, John Sheilds, George Shannon, John Potts, John Baptiste Le Page, John B. Thompson, William Werner, Richard Windsor, Peter Wiser, Alexander Willard, Joseph Whiehouse.

Civilian Interpreters: George Drouillard and Toussaint Charbonneau.

they stopped at an army fort. There they hired another civilian—George Drouillard, an experienced hunter who was an expert in Indian ways and spoke several Indian languages. It was one of their best appoint-

THE LOUISIANA PURCHASE

In 1682, when Robert Cavelier, Sieur de La Salle, became the first European explorer to travel down the Mississippi River to the sea, he claimed the entire area drained by the river for France. He named it Louisiana in honor of King Louis XIV. France retained ownership until 1762, when it ceded the vast territory to Spain. In 1800, Napoleon Bonaparte, then the leader of France, took it back under the terms of the Treaty of San Ildefonso with Spain.

That caused great concern in the United States, because it put France, a powerful nation, in control of the busy port of New Orleans. To prevent any interruption in trade, President Thomas Jefferson sent Robert R. Livingston to Paris to propose the purchase of New Orleans. After months of negotiation, Napoleon made a surprising offer: to sell not only New Orleans, but the entire Louisiana territory. The Americans quickly agreed. The price was $15 million.

But there was on obstacle: Spain still retained formal title to the land. Two complicated diplomatic actions followed. On November 30, 1803, in New Orleans, France received the colony from Spain. Twenty days later, France surrendered it to the United States.

A similar ceremony took place in St. Louis early in 1804. On March 9, the Spanish flag was lowered and the French flag raised. On the following day, the French flag came down and the Stars and Stripes went up. One of the witnesses was Captain Meriwether Lewis on the eve of his departure on the Lewis and Clark expedition.

ments. Drouillard became the expedition's chief scout, hunter, and interpreter.

In November and early December, they floated down the Ohio to the Mississippi River and paddled up to St. Louis. At that time, St. Louis, a village with a population of slightly more than one thousand, was not part of the United States. It was the key settlement of the upper Louisiana territory owned by Spain.

Lewis called on the governor, who politely ordered him not to camp on the Spanish, or west, side of the river. So Lewis sailed up to the Wood River on the American side of the Mississippi, opposite the junction of the Mississippi and Missouri Rivers. He established winter quarters there, called Camp Dubois.

During the winter, Lewis and Clark completed their preparations: They bought supplies in St. Louis, overhauled their boats, and drilled the men. They also completed their roster—a total of twenty-five soldiers and twenty civilian boatmen, guides, and hunters. Three of the soldiers were appointed sergeants: Charles Floyd, Nathaniel Pryor, and John Ordway, who was named first sergeant, to be in charge when Lewis and Clark were absent.

Lewis left the camp frequently to buy supplies in St. Louis. He was there on March 10, 1804, when the Louisiana Territory was formally transferred to the United States as the last step in the Louisiana Purchase.

Only one obstacle remained before the expedition left—Clark's official new commission in the army. When it arrived, it was a bitter disappointment. Lewis had promised Clark the rank of captain, but when the document came from Washington he was appointed only a lieutenant.

Lewis ignored the commission. He called Clark captain and so did the men. Just as he had promised, they shared command of the entire expedition. From all accounts, they got on splendidly.

THREE

The Expedition Starts

The expedition finally started on Monday, May 14, 1804. Clark wrote in his journal, with his typically erratic spelling:

Rained the fore part of the day. I determined to go as far as St. Charles a french Village 7 Leag[ues] up the Missourie, and wait in that place until Capt. Lewis could finish the business to which he was obliged to attend to in St. Louis. . . . I set out at 4 oClock P.M.. and in the presence of many of the neighboring inhabitents, and proceeded on under a jentle brease up the Missourie.

The men camped at St. Charles, where they repacked their supplies in the boats to make them more riverworthy, and waited for Lewis, who had gone to St. Louis on one of his periodic trips. When Lewis arrived, the expedition was ready to go.

On May 21, Lewis wrote in his journal: "Set out at half passed

Lewis and Clark leaving St. Charles, Missouri, at the start of their expedition.

three oClock under three cheers from the gentlemen on the bank and proceeded."

At the start, the expedition consisted of the two captains, three sergeants, a crew of thirty-eight men, including soldiers and French boatmen, plus York and Seaman. They traveled in three boats. Most of the soldiers were in the keelboat, other soldiers manned the white pirogue, and eight hired French boatmen were in the larger red pirogue. Ahead of them lay a 2,500-mile-(4,000 kilometers trip up the Missouri River, then into the unknown west until they reached a river that could take them to the Pacific Ocean. Lewis estimated that the trip would take at least two years—two years cut off from army headquarters, from orders, and from any sort of communication from family and friends.

Overcoming swift currents, rocks, drifting logs, fallen trees, and sandbars, they made their way slowly upriver. Some days they covered

Seaman

Meriwether Lewis's constant companion was his dog, Seaman, a large black Newfoundland. Lewis bought him in Pittsburgh for twenty dollars in August 1803, as he prepared for the expedition.

From the beginning, Seaman was a valuable member of the expedition. He caught squirrels, which the men ate, and once he even pulled an antelope from a river, which the men also ate. He sometimes acted as a sentry, warning the men of approaching buffalo and grizzly bears.

A strong, active dog, Seaman impressed the Indians they met. One tribe offered to buy him for three beaver skins, but Lewis refused. Another tribe stole him, but Lewis sent three armed men after them, and faced with a battle, the Indians released Seaman.

Lewis's last journal entry about Seaman is on July 15, 1806. Writing about a terrible plague of mosquitoes, Lewis wrote, "My dog even howls with the torture he experiences."

After that, silence. It seems most odd that Lewis did not record what happened to Seaman. We don't know if Seaman died, strayed, or was somehow left behind as the expedition returned to St. Louis.

only four miles (6 kilometers), on a good day as many as twenty 32 kilometers). They averaged about ten miles a day.

Their biggest hurdle was the Missouri River itself, flowing downstream at a constant rate of five miles (8 kilometers) an hour, with currents even stronger when the river was narrow. To go forward, they had to move their boats upstream faster than that.

When the wind was right, it was relatively easy. But the wind failed often. Then they had three other methods of movement: rowing with oars, pushing with poles, and "cordelling"—wading in the water and pulling the boats forward with ropes. It was hard physical labor. But the men were tough, alert, strong, and well fed.

Their diet was mostly meat—an astonishing eight pounds (4 kilograms) a day per man. Every day Drouillard and other hunters went ashore seeking fresh meat, mostly deer, bear, and rabbit. The men cooked their meat in the evening, saving leftovers for the next day's breakfast and midday meal. When the hunting parties were not successful, the men ate salted pork and corn that the boats carried.

The two captains divided their duties amicably. Clark, who was more experienced on the water, mostly stayed on the keelboat, managing the men, taking constant compass readings, and estimating the distance traveled. Lewis went ashore almost every day, walking on the banks with his dog, gathering plants, taking soil samples, and noting good sites for future forts, trading posts, and settlements.

We know the details of the trip because at least seven of the men kept journals. The most detailed was kept by Clark, who recorded the many bends in the river, the number of miles covered, and the problems they faced. On June 17, for example, he wrote:

Cloudy morning wind from the S.E. we set out early and proceeded one mile & came too to make oars & repair our cable & toe [tow] rope. . . . George Drewyer [Drouillard] our hunter and one man came

Clark and his men hunting bears for meat.

in with 2 deer & a Bear . . . The party is much afflicted with Boils, and Several have the Deassentary [dysentery], which I contribute to the water. . . . The Countrey about this place is butifull [beautiful]. . . . The Ticks and Musquiters are verry troublesome.

On June 26, forty-three days and four hundred miles after its departure, the expedition reached the Kansas River (the site of today's Kansas City). About a month later, on July 21, they came to the Platte River in Nebraska. They had traveled 640 miles (1,030 kilometers).

Soon after, Lewis and Clark met members of the Oto Indian tribe— the first of about fifty different tribes they would meet. Under instructions from Jefferson to make friends with the Indians, the two captains were very careful. To impress them, they put on their full dress uniforms,

Traveling Down the River

The expedition traveled the rivers in a large keelboat, two pirogues, and many small canoes.

The name *keelboat* comes from the word *keel*, describing a strong wooden beam stretching from bow to stern, supporting wooden frames that in turn support the sides. Their keelboat was fifty-five feet (seventeen meters) long and eight feet (two meters) wide in the center. It had a thirty-two foot (ten meters) mast with a sail, to be used when wind made sailing possible. When the wind failed, the men rowed.

In addition, the expedition used two pirogues, which were flat-bottomed wooden dugout boats resembling canoes. The largest was forty-two feet long, painted red. It was propelled by seven pairs of oars. The smaller one was thirty-nine feet long, painted white, with six pairs of oars.

complete with cocked hats. The soldiers, too, put on their uniforms and paraded in front of the Indians.

Lewis made a formal speech in which he said that the country around them now belonged to the United States and that all who lived there, whether red or white, had to obey the commands of "their Great Chief the President, who is now your only great father."

Lewis and Clark meeting with Indians.

Sergeant Ordway described the meeting in his journal:

This morning the two Captains held a Counsel with the Zottous [Otos] Indians & made 6 chiefs under the american government, they all recd their medel & other presents With Great kindness &

thankfulness they all apeared to be Glad they had got free from all other powers . . . smoked and drank with us. Shook hands and parted.

Soon after it left the Indians, the expedition ran into its first major problem. A soldier, Moses B. Reed, deserted. He was soon recaptured and sentenced by a court-martial to run four times through two lines of soldiers who beat him with sticks. He was also dismissed from the army.

But an even more serious problem developed. Sergeant Floyd came down with an illness that did not respond to the crude medicines that the expedition carried. On August 20, Floyd died, probably from a burst appendix, something that even doctors back home could not have treated. He was buried on a hill overlooking the Missouri River—the only soldier to die on the entire expedition.

Shortly after, Lewis and Clark did something unusual in a military operation: they called an election to select a sergeant to replace Floyd. The soldiers voted in the first American election to be held west of the Mississippi River. Patrick Gass got nineteen votes, more than any other candidate. Lewis promptly named Gass "sergeant in the Corps of volunteers for the North Western Discovery."

F O U R

The Northern Plains

As the summer drew to a close, the expedition moved north along the Missouri River into a new kind of country—the northern plains, home of the Sioux, the largest and most powerful tribe it would meet.

It was an exciting land where few Americans, other than Indians and an occasional fur trapper, had ever been. All around them were open grasslands populated by large herds of deer, elk, and buffalo. They ate well there.

But it was dangerous, too. The warlike Sioux controlled the upper Missouri River and stopped anyone who tried to go up the river. They acted as gatekeepers to the regions beyond, making fur traders who wanted to go farther in search of beaver pay fees in the form of tobacco and arms.

Lewis had instructions from Jefferson to avoid any armed confrontation. But could he? Would the Sioux be friendly or hostile?

Buffalo on the range, as portrayed by George Catlin.

At the end of August, in what is now South Dakota, Lewis and Clark had their first meeting with one branch of the Sioux, the Yanktons.

The two captains put on their dress uniforms to show that this was an important occasion. The Yanktons responded in a friendly way. Four musicians, singing and playing music, marched in front of their chiefs to meet the Americans. They even cooked a large dog as a treat for the visitors. Sergeant Pryor said it was "good and well-flavored."

Meeting the Yanktons.

After giving gifts of tobacco, corn, iron kettles, and medals, Lewis made his standard speech: that the Americans only wanted peace and trade. In reply, the Indians indicated their disappointment with the presents. They really wanted powder and ammunition for their guns—which they did not get. Despite some misunderstandings, the two sides were on their best behavior and the meeting ended peacefully.

Following his instructions to gather information about the Indians, Clark noted:

This [Sioux] Nation is divided into 20 Tribes, possessing seperate interests. Collectively they are noumerous say from 2 to 3,000 men, their interests are so unconnected that some Bands are at war with Nations [with] which other bands are on the most friendly terms.

The expedition proceeded upriver. A month later, at the end of September, it came into the territory controlled by the Lakotas, the most powerful branch of the Sioux. Their meeting took place near what is now Pierre, South Dakota.

Warned about the dangerous Lakotas, Lewis and Clark took precautions. One-third of the soldiers went ashore on guard, while the others remained on alert in the keelboat, with cannon aimed at where the Indians gathered. The two captains met the Sioux chiefs—Black Buffalo, the Partisan, and Buffalo Medicine—under an awning on the shore, beginning three days of tension.

The meetings were a mixture of peaceful talk and hostile actions. Sergeant Ordway summarized the first meeting:

Gave the 3 Chiefs niew meddals & 1 american flag. Some knives & other Small articles of Goods & Gave the head cheif the Black Buffalow a red coat & a cocked hat & feathe. . . . We had no good interpreter but the old frenchman could make them understand tollarable well but they did not appear to talk much until they had got the goods, and then they wanted more, and Said we must Stop with them or leave one of the pearogues with them as that was what they expected.

That led to an armed confrontation. Three Indians seized the pirogue's rope. Others drew their bows and arrows. Lewis ordered his men to load their weapons. Ordway described what happened next:

Capt Clark used moderation with them told them we must and would go on and would go. that we were not Squaws but warriers.

the chief sayed he had warriers too and if we were to go on they would follow us and kill and take the whole of us by degrees.

As the two armed groups faced each other, they continued to talk through interpreters. At one point, Clark held out his hand to the chiefs in a gesture of peace, but they refused to take it.

It was a tense moment, and the slightest miscalculation would have led to a battle. The whites, who were better armed, were nevertheless at a disadvantage. Outnumbered by at least ten to one, they probably would have been massacred.

But neither side wanted to fight. For Lewis and Clark it would have meant possible defeat and the end of the expedition. For the Sioux, it would have meant making an enemy of the new government of the United States.

Keeping their arms at the ready, the soldiers retired to their pirogues and keelboat. The Indians watched but did not interfere.

Then one of their chiefs, Black Buffalo, waded out into the river. Instead of being hostile, though, he indicated that he and some others wanted to sleep aboard the keelboat. Lewis and Clark agreed—and the confrontation was over.

On September 28, as Lewis and Clark prepared to leave, they faced another showdown. A large number of well-armed Lakotas gathered on the shore. Some grabbed the ropes holding the boats to prevent them from leaving, demanding more tobacco.

Lewis refused. After a brief argument, Clark threw a package of tobacco to the Indians on the shore. Not satisfied, Black Buffalo told him that they would be free to go only if they left more tobacco. Lewis, angry at this last demand, nevertheless threw more packages of tobacco to the Indians. They dropped the ropes holding the canoes— and the expedition departed peacefully.

As the days grew shorter and the weather colder, the expedition moved smartly north. All around the men, the grasses on the plains began to change into the golden brown of autumn. On both shores, elk and buffalo were moving south to their wintering grounds. Overhead, Canada geese, swans, and ducks flew south, too.

As the boats made good time in the river, Lewis walked on the land, carrying his journal so that he could describe the plants, animals, and the soil around him.

Soon, in early October, the expedition reached the lands of the Arikara Indians. Once a mighty nation, the Arikaras had been devastated by smallpox. With no immunity from the disease, the population had dwindled from about thirty thousand to perhaps a few thousand.

The Arikaras, a proud and friendly people, welcomed the visitors. Unlike the Sioux, who were hunters, the Arikaras were farmers, growing squash, corn, beans, and tobacco. Sergeant Gass said the Arikaras were "the best-looking, most cleanly, most friendly and industrious Indians I have ever seen on the voyage."

They were pleased with the gifts Lewis gave them, but their major interest was York, Clark's servant. They had never seen a black man before. They examined him from top to toe, even wet their hands and tried to wipe his black color off.

York enjoyed their attention. Playing with the children, he told them that he really was a wild bear, captured and tamed by Clark. He caused such a commotion that Clark finally told him to stop because he "made himself more turibal [terrible] than we wished him to doe."

After both sides made pledges of peace, the expedition left. On the way north, it encountered its first grizzly bear and the first snow of the season. With winter coming, Lewis and Clark knew they could not reach the headwaters of the Missouri River before it froze. They decided to camp for the winter among the Mandan Indians, north of what is today Bismarck, North Dakota.

Indians testing York's black skin, as painted by Charles Russell.

Even though the Mandans, like the Arikaras, had been devastated by smallpox, they maintained a large trading complex. In 1804, when the expedition stopped there, it was the largest concentration of Indians in the West—more than four thousand people in five neighboring villages, two of Mandans and three of the Hidatsa, their allies.

Every fall, other Indians arrived to trade horses and buffalo hides for corn and other crops grown by the Mandans. Canadians from the North West Company and the Hudson's Bay Company, as well as Americans from St. Louis, came to buy furs and buffalo hides.

The Mandans welcomed Lewis and Clark warmly. Lewis made his usual speech about the Americans' desire for peace and trade. He dis-

36

tributed presents of medals, coats, and hats. The Mandans seemed to be happy that the expedition planned to stay the winter with them.

On November 2, the men began to build a fort made of cottonwood logs. The fort consisted of two rows of huts, with outside walls eighteen feet (five meters) high. Two weeks later the soldiers moved in, just in time to protect themselves against the cold and snow. For the next few months, the temperature frequently dropped to ten (-23° Celcius) and twenty (-28.9° Celsius) degrees below zero.

The two captains kept the soldiers busy during the cold winter. They cut wood to keep warm, went hunting with the Mandans for food, repaired their equipment, and built six new canoes to use when the expedition resumed in the spring.

For Lewis, it was time to write a report to President Jefferson. At his desk in a smoky room in the fort, he copied astronomical readings taken along the river and wrote detailed observations of the Indians they had met and their languages, as well as descriptions of plants and animals. He prepared animal and bird skeletons for shipment back to Washington.

Lewis also made an important addition to the expedition. He hired Toussaint Charbonneau, a French Canadian, as a cook and interpreter. Charbonneau was a fur trader who lived among the Hidatsa along with his two wives, both teenaged Shoshone, or Snake Indians, who had been captured by the Hidatsa years before.

One of those wives, Sacagawea, would accompany the expedition to the Pacific Ocean. She, not her husband, would turn out to be one of the most valuable contributors to the success of Lewis and Clark.

Sacagawea, as she might have looked, painted by a later artist.

FIVE

Sacagawea

Sacagawea is one of the most famous women in American history. In the year 2000, the United States government issued a new, gold-colored one-dollar coin to commemorate her. A statue of Sacagawea holding her baby boy stands near the state capitol in Bismarck, North Dakota. She and her son are also depicted in a monument to Lewis and Clark at Fort Benton, Montana. State parks, rivers, lakes, and even a mountain (Sacajawea Peak, 9,833 feet (2,997 meters) high, in north-eastern Oregon) have been named after her.

Despite her fame, we know very little about Sacagawea's life, except for her role in helping to make the Lewis and Clark expedition a success. For example, no portrait of her was made during her lifetime, but artists have depicted their ideas of what she looked like in paintings and statues.

The most that historians have been able to discover is that she was

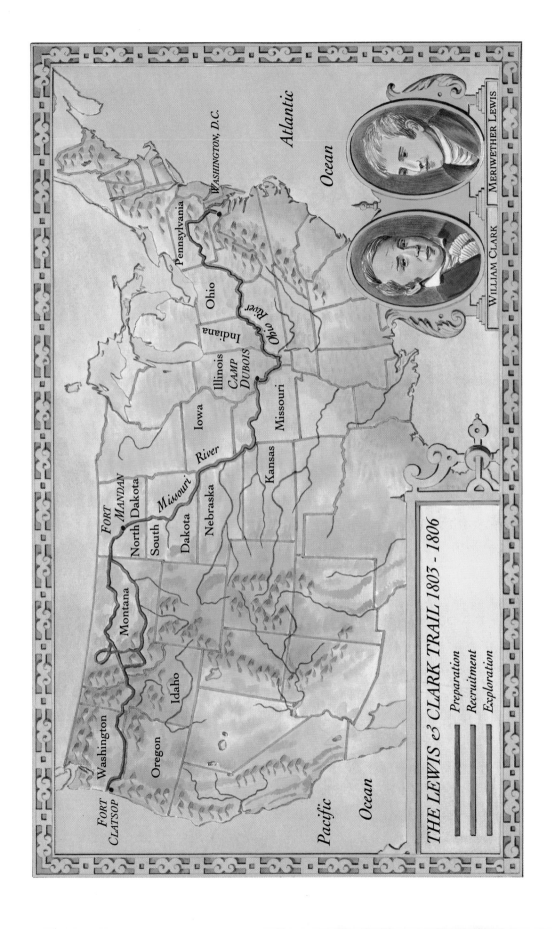

THE LEWIS & CLARK TRAIL 1803 - 1806

Preparation
Recruitment
Exploration

MERIWETHER LEWIS

WILLIAM CLARK

Atlantic
Ocean

Pacific
Ocean

WASHINGTON, D.C.

Pennsylvania

Ohio

Indiana

Ohio River

Illinois

CAMP DUBOIS

Iowa

Missouri

Missouri River

Kansas

Nebraska

South Dakota

North Dakota

FORT MANDAN

Montana

Idaho

Washington

Oregon

FORT CLATSOP

born in the late 1780s, possibly 1789. Her parents, about whom we know nothing more, were members of the Lemhi band of Shoshone Indians, who lived near the Salmon River in what is today central Idaho.

In 1800, when she was about twelve years old, she was captured by a war party of Hidatsa Indians and taken to North Dakota as a slave. When she was about fifteen years old, a forty-six-year-old French-Canadian fur trader living with the Hidatsa, Toussaint Charbonneau, either bought her or won her in a gambling game. She and another Shoshone girl became Charbonneau's companions, and were regarded as his wives.

Although Sacagawea was a Shoshone, her name came from the Hidatsa, her captors. It was a combination of two words, *sacaga*, meaning *bird*, and wea, meaning *woman*. Lewis and Clark called her "Bird Woman."

Sometimes her name is spelled Sacajawea or even Sakakawea, but the preferred spelling is Sacagawea.

She enters the pages of history at Fort Mandan in 1804, when Charbonneau was hired by Lewis and Clark. The two captains saw that Charbonneau and Sacagawea would be needed as interpreters when the expedition reached the Indian tribes to the west.

How could they be interpreters if neither of them spoke English? Lewis and Clark planned a complicated system of translation. They would speak to Drouillard, their hunter, in English. He would translate into French to Charbonneau, who would then speak to his wife in the Hidatsa language. Sacagawea, in turn, would translate into Shoshone. When the Shoshones spoke to her, the entire process would be reversed.

At the time she and her husband became members of the expedition, Sacagawea was probably about fifteen years old and about six months pregnant. On February 11, 1805, she gave birth to a son, Jean-Baptiste Charbonneau. When the expedition left its winter fort in the spring, she carried the boy in a cradle on her back. During the trip,

Sacagawea with her husband, Toussaint Charbonneau.

Clark gave the baby boy a nickname, "Pomp."

Sacagawea's very presence was a big help to the expedition when it met new Indian tribes. After one such meeting, Clark wrote in his

POMPEY'S PILLAR

The only physical evidence left behind from the Lewis and Clark expedition is a brief inscription on a monumental rock called Pompey's Pillar, on the Yellowstone River, some thirty miles (forty-eight kilometers) east of Billings, Montana. When the expedition passed by, William Clark climbed to the top of the 150-foot (forty-six meters) sandstone rock and carved on the side, *Wm Clark July 25 1806*.

He named the rock Pompey's Pillar, after the nickname that Lewis and Clark gave to Jean-Baptiste Charbonneau, the baby son of Sacagawea and Toussaint Charbonneau. In 2001—195 years after the Lewis and Clark expedition passed through Montana—President Bill Clinton named Pompey's Pillar as an official national monument.

journal: "The sight of This Indian woman . . . confirmed those people of our friendly intentions as no woman ever accompanies a war party of Indians in this quarter."

Sacagawea's role has been exaggerated by legend, but there is no doubt that she did play an important part in the expedition.

SIX

The Way West

When the ice broke up on the Missouri River at Fort Mandan in the spring, Lewis and Clark moved out.

On April 7, 1805, they dispatched Corporal Richard Warfington and a crew back down the Missouri on the big keelboat carrying five boxes of articles for President Jefferson. The boxes contained an ear of Mandan corn, four buffalo robes, a plant they described as "highly prized by the natives as an efficatious remidy in the cure of the bite of the rattle snake, or Mad dog," many animal skins and skeletons, and even such live creatures as a burrowing squirrel of the prairies, four magpies, and a prairie hen in cages.

At four o'clock in the afternoon, they cast off in their two pirogues and six new canoes, heading upstream into the vast unknown West. That night Lewis wrote in his journal:

A buffalo robe sent back by Lewis to President Jefferson.

This little fleet altho' not quite as rispectable as thos of Columbus or Capt. Cook, were still viewed by us with as much pleasure as those deservedly famous adventurers ever beheld theirs . . . We were now about to penetrate a country at least two thousand miles in width, on which the foot of civilized man had never trodden.

At this point the expedition consisted of thirty-three people: Lewis and Clark, three sergeants, twenty-three soldiers, and five civilians—Drouillard, the hunter; York, Clark's servant; and Charbonneau, his wife Sacagawea, and their infant son, Jean-Baptiste.

As they traveled, they marveled at the wildlife on the treeless plains, covered with grass in all directions. The grass supported an abundance of animals—deer, elk, buffalo, and sheep, as well as bears, coyotes, foxes, and wolves that lived on the grass-eating animals.

For many days they made good time on the river, sometimes traveling as many as twenty miles (thirty-two kilometers) a day. At other times they moved slowly, the men up to their armpits in the water, pulling the boats. On April 15, they reached the Yellowstone River and crossed into what is now the state of Montana, becoming the first white men to see that area.

Every day was an adventure—being chased by dangerous grizzly bears, observing whooping cranes and bald eagles for the first time, coping with high winds and squalls, saving supplies from overturned canoes, and roasting beaver tails and livers for dinner. "The men prefer the flesh of this anamal [the beaver] to that of any other which we are able to procure at this moment," Lewis wrote.

On May 26, Lewis got his first sight of the Rocky Mountains far in the distance toward the setting sun. He described his feelings in his journal:

When I reflected on the difficulties which this snowy barrier would most probably throw in my way to the Pacific, and the sufferings and hardship of myself and party in them, it in some measure counter-ballanced the joy I felt in the first moments in which I gazed on them.

On June 2, Lewis and Clark faced a major decision. They had arrived at a junction of two large rivers, one flowing from the northwest and the other from the southeast. "An interesting question was now to be determined," Lewis wrote that night. "Which of these rivers was the Missouri?"

All the men in the crew believed that the north fork, which was muddy like the Missouri they had traveled over, was the way to go. But both captains thought that the south fork, which flowed clear like a mountain stream, was the true Missouri.

ANIMALS AND PLANTS

As part of his instructions for exploring the new territory, President Jefferson, who had a keen personal interest in all forms of science, directed Lewis to observe the animals and plants, "especially those not of the U.S."

Obeying those instructions, Lewis, who acted as the chief naturalist of the expedition, found 178 new plants and 122 species and subspecies of animals that were not known east of the Mississippi River. He sent back to Jefferson drawings of plants, fish, birds, and mammals, as well as dried plants and seeds and the skeletons and skins of many of the animals that he found.

Among the strange new animals were the coyote—which he described as "a prairie wolf that barks like a dog"—Rocky Mountain pack rat, mountain goat, mountain sheep, black-tailed prairie dog, yellow-bellied marmot, grizzly bear, Montana horned owl, and sage grouse. He and his men also hunted and killed many familiar animals such as antelope, beaver, deer, elk, rabbit, and buffalo for food.

Among the new plants were Rocky Mountain maple, saskatoon or serviceberry, sagebrush, Oregon grape, mariposa lily, pink cleome, western larch, Osage orange, Sitka spruce, ponderosa pine, California rhododendron, and Nootka rose.

A drawing from Lewis's journal. Together Lewis and Clark recorded 178 plants and 122 animals that were new to science at the time.

Lewis's first view of the Rocky Mountains.

They made a critical decision: they would follow the south fork. The men had faith in their leaders and followed without grumbling. Lewis named the north fork the Marias, in honor of his cousin, Maria Wood.

They found out that their decision had been correct a few days later, when they came to a great waterfall on the river, as the Mandans had described. Lewis heard a welcome sound:

My ears were saluted with the agreeable sound of a fall of water and advancing a little further I saw a spray arise above the plain like a collumn of smoke . . . [it] soon began to make a roaring too tremendous to be mistaken for any cause short of the great falls of the Missouri.

To his surprise, Lewis found five separate waterfalls over a stretch of river eighteen miles (twenty-nine kilometers) long. How were they going to get around them in their canoes? The solution was easier said than done. They would have to carry the canoes and supplies by land around the waterfalls.

To do it, they built two crude wagons. For wheels, they cut a cottonwood tree and sawed it crosswise. They took down the hardwood mast of the white pirogue and cut it into the proper length for axles. Using the rest of the cottonwood, they fashioned bodies for the wagons.

It took a month of backbreaking work to construct the carts and pull them, loaded with the canoes and supplies, over the eighteen miles of rough terrain around the waterfalls. Adding to the discomfort were the summer heat and gnats, swarms of mosquitoes, and prickly pear cactuses that tore through their moccasins.

When they were finished, the two captains decided that they needed two more canoes to carry their supplies. So they chopped down two more cottonwood trees, cut out the interior wood, and made two dugout canoes.

They proceeded on in their eight canoes. On July 25, they came to the end of the Missouri River—eighteen months and 2,500 miles (4,025 kilometers) after they had started near St. Louis.

In front of them were three smaller rivers of equal size, the Three Forks that combine to form the Missouri River (south of present day Helena, Montana). They named the east fork the Gallatin, after Albert Gallatin, the secretary of the treasury; the middle one the Madison, after James Madison, the secretary of state, and the west one the Jefferson, after the president.

Sacagawea knew the area well. It was precisely there that she had been captured five years earlier by a Hidatsa war party. To Lewis and

Lewis and Clark at the Great Falls of the Missouri River.

At the Three Forks of the Missouri River.

Clark that was good news. It meant that the Shoshones could not be far away.

They decided to follow the Jefferson River. Once again Sacagawea proved most helpful. On August 8, she recognized a huge rock called Beaver Head (about twelve miles (nineteen kilometers) south of Twin Bridges, Montana). Her people lived on a river not far to the west, she said.

Lewis took a small party by land to look for the Shoshones. A few days later, he reached the continental divide at Lemhi Pass (7,372 feet [2,247 meters] elevation) at the spine of the Rocky Mountains—beyond it, the rivers flowed west to the Pacific Ocean. At the top, Lewis saw "imence ranges of high mountains still to the West of us with their tops partially covered with snow."

It was clear that the only way they could reach the Pacific was to cross those mountains on horseback. And the only way to obtain horses was if the Shoshones would trade for them.

When the expedition crossed the continental divide at Lemhi Pass into what is today Idaho, it left the area of the Louisiana Purchase and entered territory claimed by foreign nations—and the lands where the Shoshones lived.

What happened next was probably the most dramatic sequence of events of the entire expedition.

On August 13, Lewis and four of his men met their first Shoshones, two women and a man. They fled at the sight of the white men, running back to warn their village that strangers, possibly enemies, were approaching.

As Lewis went forward, he met an elderly woman with a child who could not run. As tokens of peace, he gave her some beads and mirrors. Through sign language, he asked her to conduct him to her chief.

After traveling with her for a few miles, Lewis saw a war party of sixty Indians, armed with bows and arrows and a few rifles, galloping on their horses toward him, obviously prepared for battle. Instead of setting up a defense, Lewis put down his rifle. He picked up an American flag and walked slowly toward them.

The mounted Indians halted. The woman to whom Lewis had talked showed the war party the presents she had received. Lewis described what happened next:

> *These men then advanced and embraced me very affectionately in their way which is by putting their left arm over you[r] wright shoulder clasping your back, while they frequently vociferate the word ah-hi-e, ah-hi-e, that is I am pleased, I am very much rejoiced. bothe parties now advanced and we were all carressed and besmeared with their grease and paint till I was heartily tired of the national hug.*

Lewis and his men were lucky. Outnumbered by far by the Indians,

Sacagawea meets her Shoshone relatives.

they could have been wiped out if fighting had occurred. Instead, Lewis accompanied the Indians back to their village, where they smoked the traditional pipes of peace. Through sign language, he talked to the chief, who was named Cameahwait (translated, it means One Who Never Walks).

Lewis invited Cameahwait to come back across Lemhi Pass to his base camp to meet "my brother chief"—Clark. He also told him that the American group included an Indian woman of his nation who could speak to him in his own language. Cameahwait agreed to go.

That second meeting produced a remarkable reunion. Clark described it:

Sacagawea was sent for; she came . . . sat down and was beginning to interpret, when, in the person of Cameahwait, she recognized her brother. She instantly jumped up, ran and embraced him . . weeping profusely.

Lewis and Clark named the place of the reunion Camp Fortunate.

After that, the negotiations for the horses became easier. Lewis and Clark bought twenty-nine horses, paying with knives, trinkets, leggings, mirrors, a pistol, tobacco, and ammunition.

Cameahwait gave them some bad news, though. The trails to the west through the high mountains were impassable so late in the season, with no game available for food. The one river in the area, the Salmon, was so swift and rock-filled that no canoe could possibly survive in it. Clark went out to look for himself, and he agreed.

But Cameahwait also said that one tribe, the Nez Percé, did cross the mountains each year. Although they lived on the far western slopes of the mountains, they came across on a narrow, rugged route far to the north to hunt buffalo near the Missouri River.

Lewis reached a decision: "I felt perfectly satisfyed, that if the Indians could pass these mountains with their women and Children, that we could also pass them."

S E V E N

To the Pacific

In September, the expedition left the Shoshones for what proved to be the most difficult leg of the entire trip—crossing the Bitterroot Mountains of Idaho. Their guide was an elderly Indian whom they called Old Toby.

It was rough, mountainous country, with no sign of people or roads anywhere. In some areas, the trees grew so thick that the men had to hack passages to help the horses get through. Sometimes the horses stumbled on the steep narrow path and fell backward. Rain, snow, and sleet made the going even rougher.

To make the situation worse, their food ran short. One night, camping without water, they melted snow to mix with the dried soup paste that Lewis had purchased long before in Philadelphia. The men, used to eating buffalo meat, did not like the resulting soup, so they killed a young horse for food. Sergeant Gass called it "good eating."

On September 18, Clark wrote: ". . . encamped on a bold running Creek passing to the left which I call Hungery Creek as at that place we had nothing to eate."

Lewis wrote, "I find myself growing weak for the want of food." But they had no alternative except to proceed. Several days later, they staggered down from the mountains, exhausted, weak with hunger, and suffering from dysentery.

After eleven days of hunger and backbreaking trailblazing, they had succeeded in crossing the rugged Bitterroot Mountains. They had traveled 160 miles (257 kilometers) in the most miserable of conditions.

They arrived at a village of the Nez Percé, who lived in what is today the tristate area of southeastern Washington, northern Idaho, and northeastern Oregon. It was the first encounter between the Nez Percé and white Americans, although they had been visited before by French-Canadian fur trappers, and the Indians were friendly to Lewis and Clark and their men.

The words *nez percé* in French mean "pierced nose," but there is no indication that they actually pierced their noses, although some did wear rings there. They called themselves the Nimipu, their word meaning "the people."

Lewis and Clark and their party stayed with them a week and a half, recovering their health. They traded knives, tobacco, handkerchiefs, and trinkets for roots, berries, and dried salmon.

Preparing for the final push to the Pacific, they built five new canoes by cutting down huge ponderosa pine trees, shaping the outside into the form of canoes and burning out the interior to make room for themselves and their supplies.

On October 7, the expedition set out on the Clearwater River, the currents speeding them downstream. Despite the rapids in the river, around which they had to carry their boats, they made twenty to thirty miles (thirty-two to forty-eight kilometers) a day.

The Snake River in Wyoming.

A few days later they entered the Snake River, where they continued to make good time, though here, too, there were many rapids. On October 16, they reached the Columbia River. They camped for a few days at what is today Sacajawea State Park, near Pasco, Washington.

Because there seemed to be so many dead fish lying on the banks of the river, the men were reluctant to eat even freshly caught salmon. Instead, with bells, pins, thimbles, and brass wire, they bought forty dogs from a group of Indians they met nearby and ate them. "All the men have the advantage of me," Clark wrote, "in as much as they relish the flesh of dogs."

As they passed between the last mountain range along the Columbia

gorge, the expedition gradually approached the Pacific Ocean. At several places, the men had to get out of their canoes and carry them around the dangerous rapids (many of which have now vanished behind huge dams). By November 7, Clark was able to write: "Great joy in the camp we are in View of the Ocian, this great Pacific Ocean which we been So long anxious to see."

His excitement was premature. The expedition had reached Grays Bay, a widening of the river, not the ocean. Because of rain, high winds, and flood tides, it took them ten more days to travel the last twenty miles (thirty-two kilometers) to the ocean.

Eighteen months after Lewis and Clark left St. Louis, they had

Camping along the Columbia River.

finally reached their goal—becoming the first Americans to cross the continent overland to the Pacific Ocean.

Yet at the time, there was no celebration. Without any apparent excitement, Clark simply noted in his journal, "Ocian 4142 miles from the mouth of the Missouri R."

Battered by wind, rain, and heavy tidal waters, the men needed rest more than a party. They were hungry, too. They traded goods with the Clatsop Indians for roots and fish and ate to regain their strength.

Clark took York and several other men by land to explore the north shore of the river near the ocean. They named a point at the mouth of the river Cape Disappointment because they could not see any ocean-going vessels nearby.

THE COLUMBIA RIVER

Lewis and Clark were not the first Americans to reach the Columbia River. Thirteen years earlier, on May 12, 1792, the ship *Columbia*, under the command of Captain Robert Gray, entered the mouth of the river from the Pacific Ocean. The first explorer to sail up the river, Gray named it the Columbia after his ship. By doing so, he established U.S. claims to the river and its watershed.

Several days later, Clark returned to Cape Disappointment and carved this on a pine tree:

Capt William Clark December 3rd 1805. By Land. U. States in 1804 & 1805.

Now that they had reached their goal, Lewis and Clark faced two major decisions: Should they stay there for the winter? And, if so, where?

Instead of deciding themselves, the two captains let everybody vote, including York and Sacagawea. Some historians have said that it was the first time a black slave and an Indian woman had ever voted in an American election.

The vote was decisive. They would stay on the Pacific Coast for the winter and erect a camp on the south side of the Columbia River, southwest of the present-day city of Astoria, Oregon. When their shelter was complete, they named it Fort Clatsop, after the Indian tribe that lived nearby.

EIGHT

The Return Trip

"At 1 p.m. left... on our homeward bound journey."

That was Clark's entry in his journal for March 23, 1806. After spending the winter at Fort Clatsop, the men were eager to return.

Traveling up the Columbia River against the current was hard work. It was so difficult, especially carrying their canoes around the rapids in the river, that they decided to go the rest of the way on foot, with horses carrying their supplies. They burned their canoes and bought horses from nearby Indians.

Day by day they marched overland until in early May they returned to the lands of the friendly Nez Perce. There they heard chilling news. The winter snows had been so heavy that no one could pass over the Bitterroot Mountains. They were forced to camp there and wait for favorable weather.

The Return Trip

Finally, on June 11, the impatient Lewis decided to move ahead anyway. It was a mistake. The men found twelve to fifteen feet (four to five meters) of snow in the mountains and had to turn back. It was the first time on the entire expedition that they had to retreat.

After some of the snow melted, they were rescued by the Nez Percé, who sent a group of young men to guide them through the still snowy mountains. Even with the guides, it was a long and dangerous journey. On June 30 Lewis and Clark marched down from the mountains—the worst part of their return trip over.

But before they could continue eastward, they still had some exploration to do. They divided into two major groups. Lewis led one party north to explore the Marias River almost to the Canadian border. Clark, with Sacagawea as his guide, went south to map the Yellowstone River.

A month later, on August 12, the two parties reunited at the junction of the Yellowstone and Missouri Rivers. The day before, Lewis had been wounded, shot just below the hip while out hunting. For the next several weeks, he traveled lying facedown in a canoe.

On the positive side, though, they were on the Missouri River, traveling with the current, speeding down the river. On the first day, August 13, they traveled eighty-six miles (138 kilometers); on the next day, they reached the Mandan villages where they had camped the year before.

While there, Lewis, who no longer needed interpreters, paid Charbonneau five hundred dollars and some cents for his services. Sacagawea, as his wife, received no pay. When the expedition left, Charbonneau, Sacagawea, and their son, Jean-Baptiste, stayed behind in the Mandan camp.

Clark wrote:

I offered to take his little son a butifull promising child who is 19 months old to which both himself & wife were willing provided the child had been weened. They observed that in one year the boy would

63

be sufficiently old to leave his mother & he would then take him to me if I would be so friendly as to raise the child for him.

Later, Jean-Baptiste moved into Clark's St. Louis home and was raised as a member of his family.

Accompanied by a Mandan chief who consented to go east to meet President Jefferson, the expedition sped down the Missouri. Almost every day they met boats coming upriver, carrying trappers bound for the lucrative fur trade of the Indian country.

Some of the travelers were astonished and delighted to see them—Lewis and Clark had been out of touch so long that they had been considered dead. As they neared St. Louis, local residents honored them with gun salutes.

On September 23, Clark wrote:

Ascended to the Mississippi and down that river to St.Louis, at which place we arrived at about 12 oClock. We suffered the party to fire off their pieces as a Salute to the Town we were met by all of the village and received a harty welcome from its inhabitants.

Thus ended the Lewis and Clark expedition—twenty-eight months after it started.

But its work was not complete. On the very night he arrived in St. Louis, Lewis sat down and wrote a long letter to President Jefferson, reporting his safe arrival and what they had discovered:

In obedience to your orders, we have penetrated the Continent of North America to the Pacific Ocean and have sufficiently explored the

---

Before reuniting on August 12, 1806, Lewis and Clarke led two separate parties: Lewis and his party went north to explore the Marias River; Clark went south to the Yellowstone River, pictured here.

As Lewis and Clark made their way back to St. Louis, they encountered a number of fur traders on the Missouri River.

interior of the country to affirm that we have discovered the most practicable communication which dose exist across the continent by means of the navigable branches of the Missouri and Columbia Rivers.

Then he disclosed the bad news: There was no all-water passage linking the Atlantic and Pacific Oceans. In between the Missouri and Columbia Rivers, it was necessary to travel 340 miles (547 kilometers) by land—200 miles (321 kilometers) over good roads, but 140 miles (225 kilometers) over the "tremendous Rocky Mountains which for sixty miles are covered with eternal snows."

Despite that, Lewis emphasized the economic potential of the fur trade for enterprising Americans. The area was "richer in beaver and otter than any country on earth," he wrote. And, he added, if those furs were shipped to the mouth of the Columbia River, they could reach markets in China and Europe faster than their competitors.

In early November 1806, Lewis and Clark and many of their men left St. Louis for Washington, D.C. Everywhere they passed they were treated as heroes, with banquets, balls, and parades. They arrived in Washington on December 28 to report to Jefferson.

Congress rewarded the members of the expedition with double pay and land grants. Lewis and Clark each received 1,600 acres (648 hectares) of land, the enlisted men 320 acres (130 hectares) each. Their monthly pay ranged from $5 for privates, $7 for corporals, and $8 for sergeants to $30 for Clark and $40 for Lewis.

RECOGNITION

In 2001, 195 years after the Lewis and Clark expedition ended, President Bill Clinton finally gave official recognition to the contributions of Sacagawea and York to the Lewis and Clark expedition. He awarded each of them the title of honorary sergeant in the United States Army.

N I N E

Aftermath

Meriwether Lewis

In 1807, Lewis was appointed governor of the Louisiana Territory, with headquarters in St. Louis. But it soon became clear that he was depressed and unhappy dealing with Indian affairs, army bureaucracy, and the politics of government.

He set out to return to Washington in late 1809, stopping on October 11 at a tavern south of Nashville, Tennessee. In the middle of the night, a shot was heard. Lewis was dead at the age of thirty-five of an apparent suicide. However, there is some debate about that. Some historians believe he was murdered.

Despite that unhappy ending, Lewis has come down in history as an American hero. In his book about the expedition, historian Stephen

Aftermath

E. Ambrose concluded that Meriwether Lewis was "the greatest of all American explorers."

William Clark

In contrast to Lewis, William Clark lived a long and productive life after the expedition. He resigned from the army in 1807, but was appointed a brigadier general in the militia and superintendent of Indian affairs at St. Louis. He married Julia Hancock in 1808, and they named their first child Meriwether Lewis Clark.

Appointed governor of the Missouri Territory in 1813, he commanded forces protecting the West from the British in the War of 1812. After the war he was one of the few American officials who dealt fairly with the Indians, who in turn respected him. He died in 1838 at the age of sixty-eight.

Sacagawea

Sacagawea lived in the upper Missouri Valley with her husband, Toussaint Charbonneau, who worked as an interpreter. In 1809, they went to St. Louis, where they left their four-year-old son, Jean-Baptiste, with Clark, who had promised to raise him. She also had a daughter, Lisette, who was born in 1812. It is believed that Sacagawea died later that year of a fever at the age of about twenty-three.

York

After the expedition returned, York several times asked for his freedom because of his contributions to its success. But each time Clark, his owner, refused. Finally, in 1816, ten years after the expedition ended, York succeeded in becoming a free man. He went into the freighting business in Tennessee and Kentucky, transporting supplies for others by wagon. He is believed to have died of cholera sometime before 1832.

Aftermath

The Trail Today

The Lewis and Clark Trail is one of the most popular tourist attractions in the United States today. Every year, thousands of Americans, and foreigners, too, try to follow in their footsteps, from St. Louis to the Pacific Ocean.

The entire route is clearly marked by symbols reading "Lewis and Clark National Historic Trail," established by Congress in 1978 as part of the national historic trails system administered by the National Park Service.

There are several ways to follow the trail or parts of it today:

A marker along today's Lewis and Clark trail.

70

Aftermath

By water: Although many big dams have been constructed along the Missouri and Columbia Rivers, some portions of the rivers are open to the public and their boats. Commercial boat tours are available, too.

By car: Some roads—ranging from interstate highways to unpaved dirt roads—run parallel to the route that Lewis and Clark took. They are marked with the figures of Lewis and Clark.

By foot, horseback, or bicycle: Several state parks along the trail are open to hikers and nonmotorized vehicles. Maps are available from state tourist offices.

The best single map of the entire trail is available without charge from:

National Park Service
Lewis and Clark National Historic Trail
1709 Jackson Street
Omaha, Nebraska 68102-2571
www.nps.gov/lecl
E-Mail: LECL_Administration@nps.gov

The best guide book, complete with detailed maps, historic sites, motels, and restaurants is *Along the Trail with Lewis and Clark*, written by Barbara Fifer and Vicky Soderberg, with many maps by Joseph Mussulman. It is published and sold by:

Montana Magazine
PO Box 5630
Helena, Montana 59604-9930

Timeline of the Expedition

January 1803 President Thomas Jefferson proposes expedition to explore the West, with Meriwether Lewis to command.

April 2, 1803 The Louisiana Purchase.

1803 Lewis asks William Clark to be co-commander.

May 10, 1804 United States takes formal possession of the Louisiana Territory.

May 14, 1804 Expedition leaves, traveling up the Missouri River.

Oct. 24, 1804 It reaches Mandan villages in North Dakota; Lewis decides to spend the winter there.

Nov. 4, 1804 Lewis hires Toussaint Charbonneau as cook and interpreter; he is to be accompanied by his wife, Sacagawea.

April 7, 1805 Expedition leaves Mandan camp for further exploration.

May 26, 1805 Lewis sights Rocky Mountains.

July 27, 1805 Expedition reaches Three Forks of the Missouri River.

Aug. 17, 1805 Sacagawea recognizes chief of Shoshone Indians as her brother.

Sept. 11-21, 1805 Expedition crosses the Bitterroot Mountains.

Sept. 20, 1805 It meets the Nez Percé Indians.

Oct. 6, 1805 Lewis and his men build canoes for trip down Clearwater and Snake rivers.

Timeline of the Expedition

Oct. 16, 1805 Expedition reaches the Columbia River.

Nov. 6, 1805 It sights the Pacific Ocean.

Dec. 7, 1805 It establishes winter camp at Fort Clatsop.

March 23, 1806 Expedition leaves Fort Clatsop for trip home.

Sept. 23, 1806 It returns to St. Louis, ending expedition.

Dec. 1806 Lewis reports to Jefferson in Washington, D.C.

Further Research

Books:

Anderson, Irving W. *A Charbonneau Family Portrait: Biographical Sketches of Sacagawea, Jean Baptiste, and Toussaint Charbonneau.* Astoria, OR: Fort Clatsop Historical Society, 1992.

Duncan, Dayton. *Lewis and Clark: The Journey of the Corps of Discovery.* New York: Knopf, 1997.

Faber, Harold. *From Sea to Sea, the Growth of the United States.* New York: Scribner's, 1992.

Faber, Harold: *The Discoverers of America.* New York: Scribner's, 1992.

Fifer, Barbara, and Vicky Soderberg. *Along the Trail with Lewis and Clark.* Great Falls, MT: Montana Magazine, 1998.

Least Heat-Moon, William. *River-Horse.* Boston: Houghton Mifflin, 1999.

Lomask, Milton. *American Exploration.* New York: Scribner's, 1988.

Osgood, Ernest S. and Donald Jackson. *The Lewis and Clark Expedition's Newfoundland Dog.* Great Falls, MT: The Lewis and Clark Heritage Foundation, 1986.

Websites:

Lewis and Clark Trail
http://www.lewisandclarktrail.com

Lewis and Clark's Corps of Discovery
http://www.pbs.org/weta/thewest/wpages/wpgs100/w11_008.htm

Lewis and Clark
http://www.pbs.org/lewisandclark

BIBLIOGRAPHY

Anderson, Irving W. *A Charbonneau Family Portrait: Biographical Sketches of Sacagawea, Jean Baptiste, and Toussaint Charbonneau.* Astoria, OR: Fort Clatsop Historical Society, 1992.

Ambrose, Stephen E. *Undaunted Courage: Meriwether Lewis, Thomas Jefferson, and the Opening of the American West.* New York: Simon and Schuster, 1996.

Bakeless, John. *The Eyes of Discovery: America as Seen by Its First Explorers.* New York: Dover, 1961.

Cutright, Paul Russell. *Lewis and Clark: Pioneering Naturalists.* Urbana: University of Illinois, 1969.

De Conde, Alexander. *This Affair of Louisiana.* New York: Scribner, 1976.

De Voto, Bernard. *The Course of Empire.* Boston: Houghton Mifflin, 1952.

Dillon, Richard. *Meriwether Lewis: A Biography.* New York: Coward-McCann, 1965.

Duncan, Dayton. *Lewis and Clark: The Journey of the Corps of Discovery.* New York: Knopf, 1997.

Faber, Harold. *From Sea to Sea: The Growth of the United States.* New York: Scribner, 1992.

Faber, Harold. *The Discoverers of America.* New York: Scribner, 1992.

Faber, Harold. *La Salle: Down the Mississippi.* Tarrytown, New York: Marshall Cavendish, 2001.

Ferris, Robert, editor. *Explorers and Settlers.* Washington, D.C.: National Park Service, 1976.

Fifer, Barbara, and Vicky Soderberg. *Along the Trail with Lewis and Clark.* Great Falls, MT: Montana Magazine, 1998.

Haynes, Bessie Doak, and Edgar Haynes, editors. *The Grizzly Bear: Portraits from Life.* Norman: University of Oklahoma Press, 1966.

Bibliography

Keats, John. *Eminent Domain: the Louisiana Purchase and the Making of America*. New York: Charterhouse, 1973.

Least Heat-Moon, William. *River-Horse*. Boston: Houghton, Mifflin, 1999.

Lomask, Milton. *Exploration*. New York: Scribner, 1988.

Osgood, Ernest S., and Donald Jackson. *The Lewis and Clark Expedition's Newfoundland Dog*. Great Falls, MT: The Lewis and Clark Heritage Foundation, 1986.

Quaife, Milo W., editor. *The Journals of Captain Meriwether Lewis and Sergeant John Ordway: Kept on the Expedition of Western Exploration, 1803-1806*. Madison: State Historical Society of Wisconsin, 1994.

Tomkins, Calvin. *The Lewis and Clark Trail*. New York: Harper & Row, 1965.

Thwaites, Reuben Gold, editor. *The Original Journals of the Lewis and Clark Expedition. 1804-1806*. Eight volumes. New York: Arno, 1966.

Source Notes

6 "Always remarkable for perseverance….": Stephen E. Ambrose, *Undaunted Courage: Meriwether Lewis, Thomas Jefferson, and the Opening of the American West* (Simon and Schuster, 1996), p. 27.

7 "not only to aid….": Ambrose, p. 59.

9 "Captain Lewis is brave….": Dayton Duncan, *Lewis and Clark* (Knopf, 1997), p. 8.

10 "The object of your mission….": Richard Dillon, *Meriwether Lewis: A Biography* (Coward, McCann, 1965), p. 49.

10 "In all your intercourse with the natives….": Dillon, p. 50.

10 "If therefore….": Reuben Gold Thwaites, *The Original Journals of the Lewis and Clark Expedition* (Arno, 1966), volume 7, p. 226.

12 "Dear Lewis….": Thwaites, volume 7, p. 259.

18 "Rained the fore part of the day….": Thwaites, volume 1, p. 16.

18 "Set out at half passed three….": Thwaites, volume 1, p. 25.

20 "Cloudy morning….": Calvin Tomkins, *The Lewis and Clark Trail* (Harper & Row, 1965), p. 27.

20 "their Great Chief….": Ambrose, p. 156.

20 "This morning….": Sergeant John Ordway, *The Journals of Captain Meriwether Lewis and Sergeant John Ordway* (Madison: The State Historical Society of Wisconsin, 1965), p. 77.

22 "the best-looking….": Thwaites, volume 1, p. 188.

22 "made himself more turibal….": Ambrose, p. 181.

25 "The sight of….": Duncan, p. 93

25 "This Nation is divided….": Thwaites, p. 130.

25 "Gave the 3 Chiefs….": Ordway, p. 110.

26 "Capt Clark used moderation….": Ordway, p. 111.

26 "highly prized…"" Thwaites, volume 7, p. 322.

26 "This little fleet….": Tomkins, p. 60.

27 "The men prefer….": Paul Russell Cutright, *Lewis and Clark: Pioneering Naturalists* (University of Illinois, 1969), p. 132.

27 "When I reflected….": Ambrose, p. 227.

27 "An interesting question….": Thwaites, volume 2, p.122.

27 "My ears were saluted….": Thwaites, volume 2, p. 147.

28 "immence ranges of high mountains….": Fifer, Barbara and Vicky Soderberg. *Along the Trail with Lewis and Clark*. Pg. 115.

29 "especially those not of the U.S….a prairie wolf that barks like a dog.": Cutright, pp. 399-427.

30 "these men then advanced….": Thwaites, volume 2, p. 340.

31 "Sacagawea was sent for….": Duncan, p. 135.

31 "I felt perfectly satisfied….": Thwaites, volume 2, p. 382.

32 "good eating": Duncan, p. 141.

32 "encamped on a bold….": Duncan, p. 142.

Source Notes

32 "I find myself....": Duncan, p. 142.

33 "All the men....": Ambrose, p. 197.

33 "Great joy in the camp....": Thwaites, volume 3, p. 197

34 "Ocian 4142 miles....": Ambrose, p. 305.

34 "Capt William Clark....": Thwaites, volume 3, p. 264.

36 "At 1 p.m....": Thwaites, volume 4, p. 199.

37 "I offered to take....": Thwaites, volume 5, p. 345.

37 "Ascended to the Mississippi....": Thwaites, volume 5, p. 384.

37 "In obedience to your orders...." Thwaites, volume 7, p. 334.

40 "My dog even howls....":Duncan, p. 22.

INDEX

Page numbers in boldface are illustrations.

Index

J 917.8042 FABER

Faber, Harold.
Lewis and Clark